The
Origins *of the* Creed
of The Christian
Community

The
Origins *of the* Creed
of The Christian
Community

Its History and Significance Today

Peter Selg

Floris
Books

Translated by Matthew Barton

First given as a lecture on October 19, 2017
at The Christian Community, Basel
First published in German under the title
Rudolf Steiner und das Credo der Menschen-Weihehandlng
by Verlag des Ita Wegman Instituts, Arlesheim 2017
First published in English in 2019
by Floris Books, Edinburgh

British Library CIP available
ISBN 978–178250–612–6
Printed in Great Britain by Bell & Bain, Ltd

Floris Books supports sustainable forest management by
printing this book on materials made from wood that
comes from responsible sources and reclaimed material

MIX
Paper from
responsible sources
FSC® C007785

Contents

Anthroposophy and religion

A hundred years ago, on October 19, 1917, Rudolf Steiner gave a major public lecture in Basel. Its unusual title was 'Anthroposophy does not interfere with anyone's religious confession.'[1]

There were other occasions, too, during this dramatic year of 1917 – important both for contemporary history and for the development of Steiner's work – when he addressed questions relating to anthroposophy and religion. On February 20, he suddenly and surprisingly interrupted his account of the human soul's three encounters with the powers and beings of the Trinity to say this:

> At this point I need to make an interpolation which is important and needs to be thoroughly understood by those sympathetic to spiritual science.
>
> It should not be thought that our spiritual-scientific endeavours should be a substitute for religious life and practice. Spiritual science can to the greatest degree, and especially with respect to the Christ mystery, be a support for – and a foundation of – religious life and practice. But one should not turn spiritual science into a religion, and one needs to be quite clear in one's mind that religion in its living form and when practised in a living way kindles a spiritual consciousness of the soul within the human community. If this spiritual consciousness is to become a vital presence within man, he cannot

continue to have abstract conceptions about God or Christ but he must be constantly renewed through involvement in religious practice and activity (which can take the most divergent forms for different people), in something that surrounds him as a religious environment and speaks to him out of this background. And if this religious milieu is of sufficient depth and has the means of stimulating the soul, such a soul will also come to feel a longing for those ideas that are developed in spiritual science. Moreover, if spiritual science is – as it surely is – in an objective sense a support for religious edification, the time has now come when from a subjective point of view a person with true religious feelings is driven by these very feelings also to seek knowledge. For spiritual consciousness is acquired through religious feeling and spiritual knowledge through spiritual science, just as knowledge of the natural world is acquired through natural science; and spiritual consciousness leads to the impulse to gain spiritual knowledge. From a subjective point of view one can say that an inner religious life can spur person on today to spiritual science.[2]

It is many years since Rudolf Gädeke gave a detailed examination of this important interpolation in relation to Friedrich Rittelmeyer, who was in the audience, and the origins of the Movement for Religious Renewal. Eight months later, in his Basel lecture of October 19, 1917, Steiner again picked up the theme of his key interpolation. The title of this talk, 'Anthroposophy does not interfere with anyone's religious confession,' was basically a self-quotation, though very few in his audience will have been aware of this. Almost a year previously, on October 16, 1916, Steiner had said in a lecture:

Anthroposophy does not interfere with anyone's belief; whether a person belongs to this or that confession has nothing to do with what he knows about the spiritual world, or thinks he knows, but with other circumstances of his life. The more these things are understood the more will hostility towards anthroposophy disappear.[3]

But on October 19, 1917, Rudolf Steiner did not concern himself with these varying 'circumstances of his life' and their importance for denominational differences, but instead with anthroposophy's relationship to the different confessions, and to religion altogether. He gave an account of the historical emergence of anthroposophy as modern spiritual science, as real knowledge of the spirit, *following* the development of natural science and its impact on civilisation. Unlike conventional science and academia, which subject theological traditions and religious customs to a rigorous, contextualising, relativising, and ultimately dismissive critique, Steiner highlights the ability of anthroposophy, 'to grasp the absolute value and absolute durability of religious confessions as they developed in a particular era.' He went on to say that religions would no longer emerge in our times since they presupposed a different condition of human consciousness. But it was possible, and also indispensable, to recognise the spiritual core of a religious denomination of the past, and this was a task to which anthroposophy must dedicate itself: 'An attempt is being made to live our way into them [religious confessions] not in a spirit of critique, but by taking them as they manifest, so as to understand their *raison d'être,* their value for life.' In this context, Steiner also said this:

Religious confessions speak of the spirit; and because the outcome of anthroposophic enquiry is to discern spiritual realities and spirit beings, it also converges with the religious confessions.

Unlike reductive science, which is posited on the sole reality of material substances and forces, Steiner states that anthroposophy does not primarily engage with, and ultimately disassemble, religious confession through critical analysis, but rather opens itself to them through deeper insight ('In recent times, largely because of a narrowly developed science, people have been drawn away from their experience in any particular religious confession. By contrast, as the spirit is imbued increasingly by anthroposophy they will be drawn back to it again.') In the Basel lecture we are discussing, in response to the objections to anthroposophy made repeatedly by theologians, which intensified from 1917 onward into a form of hostile propaganda, and culminated in the arson attack on the Goetheanum at the end of 1922, Steiner took up the following decisive stance:

Anthroposophy proceeds from the human being,
by developing human powers, and works into and
toward the spirit, into that realm into which religion
places its revelations. Can one be so irreligious as
to fear for the religion one has received as a truth
from divine heights if human beings make efforts –
with the powers that, as religion sees it, must after
all also come to them from the Godhead – to work
their way upward to truth about the world of spirit?
Surely the only truly religious outlook can be that
of fearlessness in this respect, knowing that religion
gives us revelations of the truth, and having no fear

that this truth will not accord with the truth that human beings themselves discover through their spirit-endowed, spirit-given powers?

As Rudolf Steiner often reiterated in other lectures, anthroposophy works out of the human I; in a certain respect, in this Michael age, it works 'on paths of will' and 'from below'. Yet, as Rudolf Steiner likewise repeatedly emphasised, divine, spiritual powers are present more than ever before in this human I and in our will for knowledge, and have been so since the last third of the nineteenth century. What was once, millennia ago, gifted from the world of spirit as revelation received by the seership of clairvoyant consciousness must now, following a metamorphosis of our powers, be acquired through inward effort. Accordingly, the truths of faith and the truths of cognition are not sundered by an unbridgeable gulf but exist in a reciprocal relation to one another. Both, religion and spiritual science, faith and knowledge, possess their own indispensable qualities, as Steiner highlighted in the Basel lecture:

> Whereas anthroposophy proceeds from the human being and strives upward into the world of spirit, the point of departure for religions has been to receive what came to them through the grace of revelation. But this acts in a different way within the human soul, filling it differently from what is created out of our own powers and endeavour. Anthroposophically oriented science of the spirit is a science, a discipline. The truths of faith inevitably engage the soul differently from the truths of cognition, the latter necessarily being the pursuit of anthroposophy. Anthroposophy cannot itself be made into a

religion. But founded on an anthroposophy that is truly understood, a real, authentic, true, unfeigned religious need will arise. The human soul, you see, is not a uniform thing but many-hued. The human soul requires diverse paths to ascend toward its goal: besides the path that engages powers of knowledge and cognition, the soul must be imbued with a warmth and incandescence in its relationship to the world of spirit such as is found in religious confession and in real religious sensibility.

In February 1917 in Berlin, Rudolf Steiner had spoken of how the practices of religion, that is, rites, sacraments and prayer, kindle the 'spiritual consciousness of the soul' and, in people today, also lead sooner or later to a longing for knowledge, and indeed, for the science of the spirit ('spiritual consciousness leads to the impulse to gain spiritual knowledge'). There too he had described anthroposophy as such as an objective support for a religious outlook and for religious practice. Now, in Basel, he suggested that, while anthroposophy could never itself create or establish a religion, and did not seek to do so, it would lead nevertheless to an 'authentic' and 'true' religious need, and in a sense culminate in religion. The practice of religion, he said, or the 'spiritual consciousness of the soul' invoked by it, engenders the soul's longing for spirit knowledge and the science that facilitates this; and this science in turn culminates in religion, so that the relationship between them becomes one of mutual interplay. Steiner concluded his Basel lecture with an epigram by Goethe from his *Zahme Xenien* (Gentle Ripostes), written in the 1820s:

He who possesses art and science
Has religion;

He who does not possess them,
Needs religion.

Steiner added:

Applied to anthroposophy, I might perhaps be
allowed to extend this saying by Goethe as follows:
If you possess anthroposophy, or the spiritual
science that blossoms from it, then you have religion
too. My fear is only that those who do not wish
to possess anthroposophy, or at least its spirit and
meaning, will not possess religion in future either.

Before the founding of
The Christian Community

This was by way of introduction to Rudolf Steiner's lecture of 19 October, 1917. I now want to move on directly to the origins of The Christian Community and the Creed, the fundamental religious confession to Christianity. (Further aspects of the relationship between anthroposophy and religion as explored by Steiner is comprehensively surveyed by Wolfgang Gädeke.)

In the late autumn of 1917, when he gave this lecture in Basel ('Anthroposophy does not interfere with anyone's religious confession') Rudolf Steiner cannot yet have known that, four years later, at around the same time of year, he would give no less than 24 lectures at the Goetheanum in Dornach on the anthroposophic view of Christianity and on the renewal of acts of worship. Around 120 people attended the lectures – primarily, though not exclusively, theologians and theology students. In his Basel lectures on 18 and 19 October, 1917, he had first announced his wish to name the St John's building in Dornach after Goethe.

> The world view of anthroposophy that I have derived from the sound and wholesome outlooks of Goethe, is one I would like to call Goetheanism, and if it were up to me, the Goetheanum would be my choice of name for the building in Dornach ... Until 1832, Goethe was a Goethean here in the physical world. If he were here today he would express himself in very different terms from how he expressed himself then.

But if something is sound and wholesome, certain underlying impulses and powers persist and carry the world view of one era on into another. When something that was germinally present, as it were, blossoms anew and bears new fruit, it can rightfully point back to this solidarity within the whole of human evolution, demonstrating indeed that it has taken up certain underlying impulses.

Four years later, between September 26 and October 10, 1921, in what had then become the School of Spiritual Science at the Goetheanum, Rudolf Steiner elaborated on anthroposophy's necessary contribution to the future of practical Christianity in terms of specific religious practice. As in 1917, he placed chief emphasis on the attainment of supersensible knowledge, and the benefits accruing from this for civilisation's progress, as the key and in some respects *only* mission of anthroposophy, or the anthroposophic movement. The goals of anthroposophy were for him nothing other than research and enquiry ('I say this as an anthroposophist'). Here Steiner was as sceptical as he had been at the end of his Basel lecture about the future of religious life and Christian practice *without* the findings and support of modern science of the spirit. On the afternoon of October 6, 1921, he cited the example of the Old Catholic Church which had been founded half a century before (1870) in protest against the papacy and the Roman Catholic Church's hunger for power:

These are understandable human reactions against the corrosive processes at work: human reactions which, it seems to me, bear within them the seed of potential transformation, even if that cannot be immediately or directly realised. But the existing churches – well, I cannot say much about the way they will go; things are going downhill fast, and I cannot conceive of things being different.[4]

By the 'seed of potential transformation' Steiner meant the possibility and need to infuse the spiritual substance of Christianity, and its rites and forms of worship, with the modern science of anthroposophy as the further development of Goetheanism. Thus Christianity could be resurrected in a new form. In Basel in 1917, he had spoken of the 'full justification', and 'the absolute value and durability' of religious confession, and indirectly also of the rites and sacraments of Christianity, *under certain preconditions*. But without the initiation of 'transformation', he foresaw only processes of corrosion, with things 'going downhill fast'; and in fact he saw such processes already actively at work. As expressed around Michaelmas 1921, they could be prevented, and indeed turned into their opposite, only by a 'transformation' founded on modern, spiritual-scientific insights.

First reading of the Creed
of The Christian Community

Many theologians who longed for such transformation had gathered in the White Room of the Goetheanum, some of them fully committed to bringing it about. On October 4, 1921, during this lecture series, Steiner elaborated the ritual of a Sunday service for children as well as a Christmas children's service and the bases of a new confirmation ritual. On the following day, he presented and explained the wording of a new service of baptism, and a day later, the words and enactments of the new mass ('My dear friends, I would now like to speak of something that could become a ceremony of the missal sacrifice; in particular, I want to show how we can move toward such a ceremony if we take account at the same time of the consciousness of modern humanity, which must always be the point of departure for the observations that I unfold before you here.').

Rudolf Steiner spoke about the Reading of the Gospel and at length about the whole Offertory in its old and new wording, and ended his lecture by referring to the Creed, the 'confession of faith' inserted into the mass between the Gospel Reading and the Offertory. He read this in its traditional form ('I believe in the one God ...') and announced that he would discuss this further in the following days ('Today I only wanted to acquaint you with the Creed that belongs to this old text [of the mass] which I have read out').

On October 7 he spoke about the Transubstantiation

and the Communion, without referring again to the Creed. At the end of the afternoon discussion on the same day, which had touched on many questions, Christian Geyer, a Protestant who was Friedrich Rittelmeyer's close companion in Nuremberg, and an important theologian and preacher, asked for more about the Creed since he and several other colleagues had to leave the next day. (the course was originally to have ended on October 8): 'Would it be presumptuous of me to ask if you could perhaps indicate, at least in outline, what form the Creed will take?' Rudolf Steiner agreed to this, though not until the following day ('Tomorrow. It's no longer possible to continue now. Tomorrow, yes we can.')

Christian Geyer was still present the next morning, Saturday October 8, and heard Steiner's comments on this and his reading of the new text of the Creed. Kurt von Wistinghausen reported this in his memoirs as follows:

> When he read [the text] out to us, we realised
> that something fundamentally new had arisen. A
> decisive era had begun in a process of development
> lasting two millennia. And we recognised that this
> text, which, like a trumpet fanfare, initiates a whole
> new Christian era – perhaps with even more clarity
> than the Act of Consecration of Man – was one that
> Dr Steiner had written down in a single night as
> if he needed only to read and transcribe it from a
> supersensible inscription.[5]

It is not at all certain, in fact, that the text was actually written down during the preceding night in response to Geyer's request. There is much to suggest that Steiner had himself already intended to speak of the Creed in its new form, but not at the end of a long afternoon of discussions. After he had read out the whole text, and then its separate sections, Christian Geyer asked Steiner, at the end, to recite the text in its entirety once again. According to reports by Gerard Klockenbring, Geyer was almost overcome and spoke of humanity's inevitable 'jubilation' at the gift of this new Creed, which from now on would be available to it as part of the Act of Consecration of Man.

> An almighty divine being, spiritual-physical, is the
> Ground of existence of the heavens and of the earth
> who goes before his creatures like a Father.
>   Christ, through whom human beings attain the
> re-enlivening of dying earth existence, is to this
> divine being as the Son born in eternity.
>   In Jesus the Christ entered as man into the earthly
> world.
>   The birth of Jesus upon earth is a working of the
> Holy Spirit who, to heal spiritually the sickness of
> sin within the bodily nature of mankind, prepared
> the son of Mary to be the vehicle of the Christ.
>   The Christ Jesus suffered under Pontius Pilate the
> death on the cross and was lowered into the grave of
> the earth.
>   In death he became the helper of the souls of the
> dead who had lost their divine nature.
>   Then he overcame death after three days.
>   Since that time he is the Lord of the heavenly
> forces upon earth and lives as the fulfiller of the
> fatherly deeds of the Ground of the World.
>   He will in time unite for the advancement of
> the world with those whom, through their bearing,
> he can wrest from the death of matter.
>   Through him can the healing Spirit work.

Communities whose members feel the Christ
within themselves may feel united in a church
to which all belong who are aware of the health–
bringing power of the Christ.

They may hope for the overcoming of the sickness
of sin, for the continuance of man's being, and for
the preservation of their life destined for eternity.

Yes, so it is.

Finding the words
for the new Creed

On the morning of October 8, 1921, Rudolf Steiner emphasised that the old version of the Creed no longer offered people what had originally been alive in it, and this had necessitated a 'retranslation founded on anthroposophic insight'. He said he had attempted 'to express what can truly be promulgated today'. Someone, he said, who possessed anthroposophic knowledge could 'put their name' to every word of the new phrases of the Creed:

> What I have summarised here you can regard as something whose every word – if words are accorded their true inner value – can be endorsed as intrinsic to anthroposophic insight.

The Creed as such, in its spiritual content – as Steiner accentuated elsewhere – was *'spiritually inviolable'*.

As mentioned previously, in his memoirs Kurt von Wistinghausen recorded the view that Rudolf Steiner had written down the wording of the new Creed during the night of October 7 to 8, 1921, following the request from Christian Geyer, 'as if he needed merely to read and transcribe it from a supersensible inscription'. I believe that we can and must also question Wistinghausen's 'merely', though he did not intend it in any trivialising sense. What is certainly true is that Rudolf Steiner did not compose some arbitrary new text, but took his lead from a spiritual reality that informed the very wording, as can be seen clearly from some of his brief expositions

– to which I will return. On the other hand, we must consider that, by his own account, he had to wrestle considerably with the wording (and thus by no means 'merely to read it' from a spiritual script). He spoke to the theologians on October 8 of the difficulty he had experienced in putting into words 'what today can be learned from its primary source in worlds of spirit'. This was not meant in general terms but specifically in relation to the contents of the Creed, and the Creed itself. He said it was 'extremely difficult' to 'even begin to find the words into which must be compressed what can really arise only as one develops world-encompassing anthroposophic knowledge.'

One day previously, on October 7, when speaking of the Transubstantiation and Communion – in the form of their new wording – he emphasised that the whole 'meaning of Christianity' certainly lived in the ritual of the mass; and he went on: 'The gospel must live in every single word of the rite, must be alive in it; and without this life of the living gospel, the rite would be impossible.' He asked his listeners to attend to the differences between the 'old text' and the ritual text that was 'possible today', but with the following proviso:

> But it is assuredly also very clear how it is almost impossible to really give form to the full, tangible experiences with a mere translation, even if it attempts to return to the old words their intrinsic value. And this is because the real meaning of the original words has been lost, in fact, for all modern civilisation. Today we no longer live within the life that words once possessed. They have become mere signs or ciphers for us. And we no longer inwardly hearken to the words. Our feeling for the sounds of

words has faded for us into a mere means of recall,
into a sense of them as ciphers.

Rudolf Steiner had to meet and deal with this situation.
It was necessary, he emphasised, to choose words 'with
real inner conscientiousness', and, 'feeling one's way into
these words, entering fully into them, actually has to be
a living process.'

What Rudolf Steiner said here related, and still relates,
it seems to me, both to his re-creation of the text *and*
to its reception by us. The listener, too, must try to
develop a new relationship to the words 'with real inner
conscientiousness' and 'enter fully into them'. Thus we
must pass through a *'living process'* with and through them.
At the end of his short introduction, directly before he
read the text, Steiner then forcefully reiterated:

> I have tried by all possible means to find incisive
> words for what an anthroposophic conviction must
> regard as necessary to such a Creed. But please do
> not think that this has been wholly successful in my
> view. It is quite clear to me what needs to be said,
> but what needs to be said is extraordinarily hard to
> put into words, for our words have largely lost their
> intrinsic value and have become outward symbols
> and ciphers. Even if some of what I read now should
> shock you, I beg you to regard it – with this proviso –
> as a possible anthroposophic Creed.

Thus he saw the wording of the Creed as a provisional,
not yet conclusively 'successful' text. According to Kurt
von Wistinghausen, his listeners saw it differently: they
immediately experienced it as something 'fundamentally
new', coming at a crisis point in a 'process of development

over two millennia', and felt that it was couched in the language of an 'entirely new Christian era':

An almighty divine being, spiritual-physical, is the ground of existence of the heavens and of the earth who goes before his creatures like a Father.

Christ, through whom human beings attain the re-enlivening of dying earth existence, is to this divine being as the Son born in eternity.

In Jesus the Christ entered as man into the earthly world.

The birth of Jesus upon earth is a working of the Holy Spirit who, to heal spiritually the sickness of sin within the bodily nature of mankind, prepared the son of Mary to be the vehicle of the Christ.

The Christ Jesus suffered under Pontius Pilate the death on the cross and was lowered into the grave of the earth.

In death he became the helper of the souls of the dead who had lost their divine nature.

Then he overcame death after three days.

Since that time he is the Lord of the heavenly forces upon earth and lives as the fulfiller of the fatherly deeds of the ground of the world.

He will in time unite for the advancement of the world with those whom, through their bearing, he can wrest from the death of matter.

Through him can the healing Spirit work.

Communities whose members feel the Christ within themselves may feel united in a church to which all belong who are aware of the health-bringing power of the Christ.

They may hope for the overcoming of the sickness of sin; for the continuance of man's being; and for the preservation of their life destined for eternity.

Yes, so it is.

After reciting the whole text of his 'translation', Rudolf Steiner went through it phrase by phrase comparing and contrasting it with the – or rather *one* – old version of the Creed. In doing so, he repeatedly said things like, 'I cannot find a wording other than this,' 'This is the only text possible in relation to St John's Gospel,' 'Well, this really has to be expressed like this,' 'These are naturally ideas that have to be given in *this* way,' 'I had to express this by saying ...'

In my view, Kurt von Wistinghausen rightly understood his words about 'finding' the text ('I cannot find a wording other than this ...') as a pointer to the quality of spiritual reception of something objective, a 'spiritual inscription' that could be 'read'. Without doubt he was here underscoring *one* important aspect of the process of Inspiration. However, the phrase 'I had to express this by saying ...' shows another, very much opposite perspective – that of autonomous, reformulating 'translation' work ultimately undertaken in and through personal responsibility.

It is very likely that many of the theologians would have wanted Rudolf Steiner subsequently to explain 'his' text of the Creed, word by word and phrase by phrase, commenting on the underlying content of ideas, or the anthroposophic and Christological insights underpinning each coinage. Yet Steiner did not do so, although he not only recognised the need for such 'exegesis' but also himself affirmed this. He said, rather, that years of interpretative theological study would be important and indeed indispensable for this. I would add: years of theological *and* anthroposophic study, 'for wide-ranging knowledge is in fact necessary to absorb the meaning of what a Creed can offer.'

The 'extensive research' and huge field of enquiry of which Steiner spoke in relation to textual exegesis encompassed theological study in so far as – from early Christian times – the labours of many outstanding minds in theological philosophy stood behind the simple formulations of the Roman Creed, the Apostles' Creed and what was known as the Nicene Creed: developments of thought and terminology whose substance and context it was necessary to know in order to evaluate the unique quality and expressive power of the new text. But in order to gain even deeper understanding of what determined the content of Rudolf Steiner's new text, and what made it possible, one also needed to study anthroposophic Christology including anthroposophic cosmology. This was necessary even to understand the very first sentence: 'An almighty divine being, spiritual-physical, is the ground of existence of the heavens and of the earth who goes before his creatures like a Father.'

The development of the text
of the Creed

Rudolf Steiner did not even begin to embark on such interpretative work on October 8, 1921, nor did he supply it in subsequent meetings with the theologians. Clearly he wanted them to start living meditatively and ritually with the Creed 'with real inner (linguistic) conscientiousness' and to undertake the necessary studies. He expressed his hope that priest seminaries would be established in future and, as he said explicitly, would engage in this work. In a discussion with the priests five months later, in Berlin, he referred to a further aspect of what he regarded as necessary for their understanding, saying on March 11, 1922: 'One must have ideas about the development of the Creed, and how it has been taken up in one place or another.'[6]

Steiner knew that the traditional text of the Creed had already undergone a long process of development, with many changes over the course of time: both throughout the evolution of consciousness since the beginning of the Christian era, and also through the different cultures that assimilated it. The Christian Creed had its history, which it was necessary to know. Back in January 1916 already, in a lecture in Dornach about the origins and scope of influence of the Creed in the first Christian centuries, Steiner had said briefly: 'If we study it [the Creed] in the way it was at the time, we can indeed discover that it is basically a defence against gnosis, a rejection of gnosis.' In the Creed of early Christianity, he went on, an emphasis was apparent on the importance of Christ becoming man, his passage into the material world, and accentuation of the principle of the Trinity, as opposed to the spiritualising tendencies of the gnosis. Thus early Christianity, or its leading theologians, had, with the Creed, erected 'barricades against the gnosis':

> We can see an incredible striving in that time with regard to how the spirit is connected with the material aspect which is spreading in the world, how the spirit can be thought as being connected with matter, the Trinity can be thought as being connected with external matter as it spreads. That is what is sought, intensively sought. But if we consider all the things that live in the Apostolic Creed, which today has become totally incomprehensible, we have to say: in it there still lives an echo of the old clairvoyant concepts which is dying out, and so the matter does not acquire the old living forms which it could have acquired if the Trinity and the Apostolic Creed had been understood with the previous clairvoyant concepts, but instead it represents a start in grasping matter together with the spirit.[7]

Christian Community works on the Creed

'One must have ideas about the development of the Creed, and how it has been taken up in one place or another.' I would here like to recall Adolf Müller (1895–1967), one of the priests who later especially took up this task of research which Steiner touched on in March 1922 in Berlin: enquiry into the 'original establishment' and subsequent 'assimilation' of the Creed. Müller, a Protestant minister in south-east Germany, joined the founding circle, and was ordained by Friedrich Rittelmeyer on September 16, 1922, in the White Room. Later he worked as a priest in Berlin. He was a cultured and quiet bachelor, who continued to celebrate in secret even during the time of the Nazi prohibition (1941–45), and faithfully cared for his congregation.*

As early as 1932, ten years after Steiner had spoken of this task of developing 'ideas' about the development and uptake of the Creed, Müller published his book on the developmental stages of the Creed, and subsequently continued to work further on it. There he surveyed ground-breaking theological and historical publications on the Creed, including the basic studies by Adolf von Harnack (1892), Ferdinand Kattenbusch (1894–1900),

---

* During the prohibition he was able to earn his living by working in a factory. In the war when Berlin was heavily bombed, he continued faithfully visiting members and friends. After the wall was built in 1961, he lived in difficult circumstances in a ruined house in East Berlin near the centre of the city, and was thus separated from most of the Berlin Christian Community. For its gatherings, this split-off eastern part of the Berlin congregation used a room in the backyard of a house not far from the ostentatious, newly built Karl-Marx-Allee (until 1961 called Stalin Allee). Adolf Müller worked there until his death in 1967.[8]

Friedrich Loofs (1902) and Karl Thieme (1914). With the aid of anthroposophy he delved more deeply into these, in the quest to uncover the 'trail of *inner* development' as he emphasised. In the introduction to his book in 1932, he described the ethos that had governed him: 'Even the academic treatment of a ritual text such as the Creed ... must hearken to the call that Moses once received: "Take off your sandals, for the place where you are standing is holy ground".' In 1974, his colleague Arnold Suckau reissued an expanded edition of Müller's posthumous work on the subject. Alongside a ground-breaking essay by Rudolf Frieling and Kurt von Wistinghausen's monograph of 1963, Müller's books are the most important fundamental studies published on the Creed by Christian Community priests, and entirely in line with the task to which Rudolf Steiner referred. Below I wish to briefly summarise some of Müller's findings as they relate to the context of these present observations.

Based on expositions by Rudolf Steiner and Rudolf Frieling,[9] Adolf Müller described early, pre-Christian confessions of faith as an attempt at 'assimilation into consciousness' (Frieling) of initiation experiences. In his book, *Christianity as Mystical Fact,* Rudolf Steiner had written of how those who underwent initiation afterwards recorded 'experience of the most sublime kind': 'I was dead – I was in the underworld – I arose again from the dead.' Rudolf Frieling commented on this: 'It seems to have been part of the initiation ritual for the one who returned to give a testimony of what had occurred.' According to him, this pre-Christian spiritual confession was an 'account drawn from profoundly personal experience'. Like Adolf Müller, Frieling referred here, among other things, to Book 11 of the *Metamorphoses* by the North African writer Apuleius, where the following more literary account is given of Isis initiation:

I approached the very gates of death and set on foot
on Proserpine's threshold, yet was permitted to
return, rapt through all the elements. At midnight
I saw the sun shining as if it were noon; I entered
the presence of the gods of the under-world and the
gods of the upper-world, stood near and worshipped
them.[10]

Rudolf Frieling also cited in this context the profession
by John, writer of the Apocalypse. John had a vision of
the Christ exalted, with seven stars upon his right, and
the shining countenance of the sun, and heard the speech
of Christ: 'I was dead, and now look, I am alive for
ever and ever! And I hold the keys of death and Hades.'
(Rev 1:18).

Here the experiences of Christ and his initiated pupil
merged in relation to the Mystery of Golgotha, the
passage through death and the reality of the Resurrection.
And, as Adolf Müller emphasised, it was precisely this
that formed the beginning of the content of the Christian
confession of faith by human beings: 'The Creed is
a conceptually organised essence of human spiritual
experiences in witness of the appearance of Christ' – this
appearance encompassing the Baptism, Crucifixion and
Resurrection.

The Creed as preparation
for baptism

In the third century, first testimonies emerged about how Christianity's original confession of faith had arisen within the circle of the disciples from the Whitsun spirit that held sway amongst them. According to this tradition, the twelve articles of the Creed go back to the circle of the twelve members who had accompanied his sojourn on earth and had eventually drawn close to understanding him. St Pirmin, who very probably was a Celtic monk from Ireland, and who founded the monastery of Reichenau (724), spoke of how the text originated as Whitsun inspiration through the Paraclete, the Holy Spirit of which Christ had said in the farewell discourses to his disciples on Maundy Thursday, that in future it would 'teach' them everything:

> And I will ask the Father, and he will give you
> another advocate to help you and be with you forever
> – the Spirit of truth ...
> But when he, the Spirit of truth, comes, he will
> guide you into all the truth. He will not speak on
> his own; he will speak only what he hears, and he
> will tell you what is yet to come. He will glorify
> me because it is from me that he will receive what
> he will make known to you. All that belongs to the
> Father is mine. That is why I said the Spirit will
> receive from me what he will make known to you.
> (John 14:16f, 16:13–16)

The Creed concerns Christ becoming man, the death and Resurrection, the past, the present and the future as Christology sees it: 'He will glorify me because it is from me that he will receive what he will make known to you.' Pirmin and his predecessors – though not modern theologians – found in the Creed, right into its linguistic form, an expression of precisely this process of teaching and revelation. Their point of departure was that the wording of the Creed had been created by the group of disciples together, speaking as it were with twelve voices. It began with the reference to the Father by Peter (first article), which John took up and led over to the Son (second article), and so on, through to Thomas, to whom, because of his particular experiences on Low Sunday ('Reach out your hand and put it into my side' John 20:27), it fell to speak of the Resurrection. The *Apostles' Creed,* in this interpretation, as apostolic confession, belonged not only to early Christian tradition but was for over a millennium an integral part of Christian art until it increasingly succumbed to modern critiques and was eventually dismissed as a legend.

The wording of the Creed very probably first arose in the second century, though it is found in its entirety in written form only in the first half of the fourth century (AD 337), in a letter in Greek in which Marcellus of Ancyra, a deposed bishop, sought to prove his orthodoxy to Pope Julius in Rome. The literature tells us that the Creed was very probably conceived in Greek, and only assumed its Latin form in Rome where (according to Rufinus of Aquileia) Peter had brought it.

It is important to know that the early Christians did not include the spoken Creed as part of the mass but that it formed part of (adult) baptism, and indeed, possessed a decisive importance there as an 'initiation into Christianity' (Frieling). Baptism marks one's acceptance into the community of Christians, and in early Christianity it still possessed qualities resonant of an act of initiation, and thus also of a particular form of spiritual experience. It was regarded and designated as 'illumination', an occurrence involving the Holy Spirit, and it was primarily conducted during Easter night, following long and intensive preparations, the catechumenate. The wording of the Creed and of the Lord's Prayer, both of which were long kept secret, was only given to the candidates for baptism during the course of their preparation.

The Creed was given two and a half weeks before Easter, on a Wednesday in Lent. At this ceremony, the Gospel concerning the healing of the man born blind (John 9) was read out; their own eyes were then to be opened (their 'illumination') at Easter. They prepared themselves for this with the Creed and the Lord's Prayer. The candidates learned the two sacred texts by heart, 'so that,' as was clear to Rudolf Frieling, 'this learning was internalised and deepened by the experience of the holy days'. At Easter, faith was to become 'seeing', endowed with the 'heart's power of vision' (Emil Bock). In the mass on Easter night, the candidates for baptism uttered the Creed, very probably by 'call and response' to the priest. The priest represented the authority of divine revelation, and the candidate for baptism responded to this. The Creed of course was not central to baptism, during the actual act of which the content of the text then became a tangible *experience,* as Adolf Müller stressed:

[During immersion in the baptismal water],
the Word that had previously been acknowledged,
became *being.* The truths and powers to which the

soul had sworn allegiance came to experience as supersensible realities. What candidates had *professed* could now be *perceived*.[11]

Thus the Holy Spirit emanating from Christ was taken up, at least in incipient form, by the human I.

The candidates for baptism prepared themselves for this experience that accompanying the release of their soul and spirit from the body during baptism by immersion. The confession of faith not only had to be uttered during the ritual of baptism but needed to have been previously fathomed and understood, in a process during which the candidate, with guidance, underwent a real inner deepening of the thinking spirit-soul. The first interpretations of the Lord's Prayer that have come down to us (by Tertullian, Origen and Cyprian) relate to the catechumenal context and originate from the beginning of the third century. No other relevant doctrinal texts relating to the Creed are extant. However both Cyprian and Tertullian knew the (or *a*) text of the Creed, as is indirectly apparent from their works. According to St Ambrose, it is important, indeed essential, for Christians to recall the Creed each day in the early morning, 'as the seal of their heart' and to safeguard their existence.

First formulation
of the Creed

To profess Christianity and Christ in any form, or in the particular form of the Creed, was existentially dangerous during that era. Kurt von Wistinghausen believed that the early Christians prayed, meditated and recited the Creed as 'primary avowal' out of their inner or inmost selves with an intensity and devotion that resembled that of the apostle Peter in Caesarea Philippi.

It is probable that Peter's Confession as it was known, played a major part in the development of the Creed. Half a year before his death, Jesus asked his disciples in northern Galilee, at a spring of the Jordan close to Mount Hermon, 'Who do the crowds say I am?' According to Luke, this question arose in a meditative context: 'Once when Jesus was praying in private and his disciples were with him, he asked them ...' (9:18). After the disciples had reported various sayings about him, he then turned to them and asked, 'But what about you? ... Who do you say I am?' Christ was here asking for a 'statement', a true 'avowal' and not for a mere opinion. At this, Peter answered, 'God's Messiah.' Or, in Matthew's Gospel, 'You are the Messiah, the Son of the living God.'

Peter's insight, his knowledge, became a confession, an insight he did not owe to his body-bound reason and his waking consciousness, but, as Christ stressed, to higher powers ('Blessed are you Simon, son of Jonah: for this was not revealed to you by flesh and blood, but by my Father in heaven' Matt 16:17). Not 'human thoughts' but 'divine thoughts' were vouchsafed to Peter at this moment, at which Christ responded with his blessing. Johannes Lenz, drawing on the Johannine philosophy of Johann Gottlieb Fichte remarked on this with a quotation from Fichte: '[A person] has but to forsake the transitory and perishable with which the true life can never associate, and thereupon the eternal with all its blessedness, will forthwith descend and dwell with him.'[12] When the breakthrough in avowal occurred in Caesarea Philippi, Christ's annunciations of his death began, and indeed, the path toward Golgotha itself, which unfolded in stages and also in a sequence of stages within the consciousness of the disciples.

Speaking the Creed at baptism, when someone entered the community of Christ, recalled this situation, and indeed internalised it. We do not know the wording of the Creed used at the act of baptism in early Christianity. The earliest form of it that has come down to us is the Old Roman Creed or the Credo Romanum which may have been in use already in the second century (when, as we know, a battle was being waged against Gnosticism).

> Credo in deum patrem imnipotentem;
> et in Christum Iesum
> filium eius unicum, dominum nostrum,
> qui natus est de Spiritu Sancto et Maria virgine,
> qui sub Pontio Pilato crucifixus est
> et sepultus,
> tertia die resurrexit a mortuis
> ascendit in caelos, sedet ad dexteram patris,
> unde venturus est iudicare vivos et mortuos;
> et in Spirituam Sanctum,
> sanctam ecclesiam,
> remissionem peccatorum, carnis resurrectionem.
>   Amen.

The Creed as a defence against gnosis

The Old Roman Credo has a simple, short text; Adolf Müller wrote of the 'Roman spirit' to which it testifies, making the confession of faith into a 'law' or 'tenet' in close affinity with legal norms of the time. *Credo in Deum, patrem omnipotentem.* There was – and remains – a glaring problem connected with this. Paul wrote to the community in Corinth, 'Where the Spirit of the Lord is, there is freedom' (2Cor 3:17). As consciousness of self consolidated with the beginning of the Christian era and the old mysteries were lost, spiritual insights receded. The situation of the macrocosmic Lord's Prayer* had by no means been entirely redressed by the fact of Christ's incarnation; our separating 'I' remained sundered from the world of spirit, we 'forgot' the 'Fathers in the heavens'. And early Christianity became progressively less spiritual as ecclesiastical power developed. We can say that 'freedom' was lost along with the 'spirit of the Lord'. The dictum or dogma of a concluded revelation became increasingly widespread, and what had once resulted from the assimilation into consciousness of spiritual insights became already in the second century the *Regula fidei,* the rule of faith, from which the faithful could only deviate at the price of being branded heretics.

In 1932 Adolf Müller wrote: 'In regard to claims of hegemony, and the intrinsic nature of dogma, we can

---

* In 1913 Rudolf Steiner spoke of a 'primal macrocosmic world prayer,' a Cosmic Lord's Prayer. See Steiner, *The Fifth Gospel.*

see that the Christian Church entered into an alliance with the Roman impulse of subjection and legislative clauses.' On the other hand, however, I believe that we cannot overlook the fact that what came into effect here was not *only* an authoritarian mode. As Rudolf Steiner highlighted in the parenthesis in the lecture of 1916 quoted earlier, great importance should be attached to what is expressed in the Creed as a defence against gnosis that turned its back on the earth, and an emphasis instead on the emphatic spiritual-*physical* incarnation of the Christ being. Nor should we underestimate the existential importance accorded to the simple Old Roman Creed as a 'seal of the heart' at a time of persecution. The *Regula fidei* (which later, in altered form, was recited in the form of a litany) can nowadays strike us as an almost abstract or legalistic dictum. But in the early centuries of Christianity it *lived* in people with inner fire and fervour. *'Credo in Deum, patrem omnipotentem.'* It lived through comprehending thinking, the 'power of heart's vision' and the confessing will of the faithful. Speaking the Creed, either aloud or silently to oneself, was seen as a deed, and in early Christian times no doubt was such. The conviction of the existence of the spiritual realm was sustained through times of persecution and oppression assuredly had something to do with the Creed.

The Nicene Creed

'One must have ideas about the development of the Creed, and how it has been taken up in one place or another.' Adolf Müller described how the Creed was received in the West in subsequent centuries (especially in Gaul and Spain) and in the East, where the diversity of its forms and variants increased. Müller characterised the text as being of fluid magnitude. He highlights developments and additions to the initially succinct content, along with the Celtic influence, that are apparent in the later Apostles' Creed, and to which are attributable important aspects that include phrases about the 'Creator of heaven and earth', the 'community of the saints', and 'eternal life'. He demonstrates the connection of these to Celtic Christianity. By its assimilation and further development in Iro-Scottish culture, the Creed gained rhythm and resonance, depth and spiritual inwardness. Previously there had been no word of Christ Jesus having 'suffered' and having actually died – rather than just being 'crucified' and 'buried' – nor of his 'descent into hell', which was only now added to the text despite the fact that it had been part of the original body of thought of Christianity.

Finally, Müller examined in great detail the eastern version of the Creed, which was known as the Nicene Creed (or Niceno-Constantinopolitan), extant in its entirety after AD 451. He emphasised the hymnal character of the version used in the eastern Church ('In the West, more uniformly configuring forces are at work, achieving a more stable form, whereas in the East we find flowing, streaming life that allows for a freer development') and the predominance of Johannine elements of wisdom and love. He also showed how the Nicene Creed advanced in the West too. From the end of the sixth century it was *sung* during worship by the congregation in Spain and Gaul before the Lord's Prayer, and at the beginning of the eleventh century (1014) was also integrated into the Roman mass. In the Nicene version, the Creed therefore first became part of the western rites.

On October 8, 1921, in the White Room at the Goetheanum, when Rudolf Steiner presented the new form of the Creed of the Act of Consecration of Man, he contrasted it with the Nicene Creed, reading the latter in the following version:

I believe in the one God, the Almighty Father, maker of heaven and earth, and of all that is, seen and unseen.
And in the one Lord, Jesus Christ, the Son of God born conjunct, who also proceeded from the Father before all cycles of time, who is God from God, Light from Light, true God from true God; originating not made, one in Being with the Father: through whom all things were made.
Who descended from the heavens for us human beings and for our salvation, who also came into the flesh from the Holy Spirit out of the Virgin Mary, and became man.
Who for us was crucified under Pontius Pilate; he died and was buried.
On the third day he rose again in fulfilment of the Scriptures,
And was raised up to heaven again and is seated at the right hand of the Father,

And he will reveal himself again to judge the living and
the dead, and his kingdom will have no end.
I believe in the Holy Spirit, the Lord and giver of life:
who proceeded from the Father and the Son, who
with the Father and the Son is at the same time
worshipped and revealed, who has spoken through
the prophets
And in the one holy catholic and apostolic Church
I acknowledge one baptism to root out wrongness, and
I hope for the resurrection of the dead, and for a life
of the world in future cycles of time
Yes, so be it.

The priest and
the Creed

Rudolf Steiner affirmed the traditional position of the Creed in the mass between Gospel Reading and Offertory – 'In fact, that is certainly the right place for it.' He said that to spiritually comprehend the Act of Consecration of Man it was necessary to grasp the connection between the whole act of worship and the Creed; modern consciousness, he said, must school itself to approach the Act of Consecration in an 'immediate' or 'primary' way. But to do so it was important, or actually essential, to begin with the Gospel and the Creed:

> First, the gospel is read, and through the Creed, the
> person celebrating the mass – the actual celebrant
> – can make a kind of response to the inspired word
> that resounds to him in the gospel.

As Steiner stressed, in the Creed the priest acknowledges what lives and resounds in him. Barely a year later, on September 17, 1922, on the occasion of the founding of The Christian Community, the first services of the Act of Consecration of Man, and the ordaining of priests, he clarified this further by stating that in the Creed, the 'human word' resounds as answer to the 'Word of God'. The priest takes off the stole and responds to God as a human being. Steiner further specifies that the Creed is spoken by the community through the mouth of the priest. Only afterwards, after this human act within the Act of Consecration of Man, does the priest's enactment as such continue.

In a certain respect, in his Creed response to the divine or cosmic Word of the Gospel, the priest as representative of the community does what the catechumen was obliged to perform in the Easter night mass of early Christianity. 'In relation to the forming of new Christian communities,' said Steiner on October 8, 1921, 'I believe that this Creed could initially create a foundation to hold the communities together through the guiding priests.' In the same context he definitively rejected ecclesiastical requirements for a confession of faith ('oath') by confirmands. To really penetrate the Creed with understanding, he said, took years of study and spiritual experience, and could not possibly be expected or even demanded of young people. It was, however, perfectly possible and reasonable for the young Confirmation candidates to hear it being spoken, at and after their Confirmation, by the priest during the Act of Consecration of Man. Referring to a fundamental law of pedagogy – the early assimilation of content that is later drawn forth again from memory and thus becomes a 'vital power' in us, Rudolf Steiner said:

> But if this relates to something like the Creed, children themselves must not be expected to believe these things, rather a feeling must be awoken in them that the person dealing with them really believes in them. We must definitely go no further than this: the person who concerns himself with children believes and knows these things, and this gives children the sense that they can eventually grow into an understanding of what this person believes. It is not possible to found and establish a community pervaded by inner truth without this feeling; but this is precisely what a Christian community must be above all.

Comparison of versions
of the Creed

As I emphasised at the outset, on October 8, 1921, Rudolf
Steiner did not interpret the Creed and his new version
of it; his work of anthroposophic enquiry culminated
instead in the form of the text that he then passed to
the theologians for their own use. To bring home the
nature of his translation work more clearly, I will now
show the various historical versions of the Creed, from
articles 1 to 12: first in the form of the Old Roman, then
the (later) Apostles', then the Nicene Creed (in the
translation used by Steiner) and finally in the Christian
Community Creed in Rudolf Steiner's own new coinage
(see table overleaf);

Old Roman Creed	*Apostles' Creed*
I believe in God, the Father Almighty;	I believe in God, the Father Almighty, creator of heaven and earth,
And in Jesus Christ, his only Son, our Lord,	And in Jesus Christ, his only Son, our Lord,
Who was born of the Holy Spirit and the Virgin Mary	Who was conceived by the Holy Spirit, and born of the Virgin Mary,
And who under Pontius Pilate was crucified and buried.	Suffered under Pontius Pilate, was crucified, died and was buried.
	He descended into hell.

Nicene Creed	Christian Community Creed
I believe in the one God, the Almighty Father, maker of heaven and earth, and of all that is, seen and unseen.	An almighty divine being, spiritual-physical, is the ground of existence of the heavens and of the earth who goes before his creatures like a Father
And in the one Lord, Jesus Christ, the Son of God born conjunct, who also proceeded from the Father before all cycles of time, who is God from God, Light from Light, true God from true God; originating not made, one in Being with the Father: through whom all things were made.	Christ, through whom human beings attain the re-enlivening of dying earth existence, is to this divine being as the Son born in eternity.
	In Jesus the Christ entered as man into the earthly world.
Who descended from the heavens for us human beings and for our salvation, who also came into the flesh from the Holy Spirit out of the Virgin Mary, and became man.	The birth of Jesus upon earth is a working of the Holy Spirit who, to heal spiritually the sickness of sin within the bodily nature of mankind, prepared the son of Mary to be the vehicle of the Christ.
Who for us was crucified under Pontius Pilate; he died and was buried.	The Christ Jesus suffered under Pontius Pilate the death on the cross and was lowered into the grave of the earth.
	In death he became the helper of the souls of the dead who had lost their divine nature.

Old Roman Creed	Apostles' Creed
On the third day he rose again from the dead,	On the third day he rose again from the dead;
Ascended to heaven and is seated at the right hand of the Father,	He ascended into heaven, and is seated at the right hand of God the Father Almighty
Whence he will come to judge the living and the dead.	From there he will come to judge the living and the dead.
I believe in the Holy Spirit,	I believe in the Holy Spirit,
The holy Church,	The holy catholic Church, the communion of saints,
The forgiveness of sin, the resurrection of the body.	the forgiveness of sins, the resurrection of the body, and the life everlasting.
Amen	Amen

Nicene Creed	Christian Community Creed
On the third day he rose again in fulfilment of the Scriptures,	Then he overcame death after three days.
And was raised up to heaven again and is seated at the right hand of the Father,	Since that time he is the Lord of the heavenly forces upon earth and lives as the fulfiller of the fatherly deeds of the ground of the world.
And he will reveal himself again to judge the living and the dead, and his kingdom will have no end.	He will in time unite for the advancement of the world with those whom, through their bearing, he can wrest from the death of matter.
I believe in the Holy Spirit, the Lord and giver of life: who proceeded from the Father and the Son, who with the Father and the Son is at the same time worshipped and revealed, who has spoken through the prophets	Through him can the healing Spirit work
And in the one holy catholic and apostolic Church	Communities whose members feel the Christ within themselves may feel united in a church to which all belong who are aware of the health-bringing power of the Christ.
I acknowledge one baptism to root out wrongness, and I hope for the resurrection of the dead, and for a life of the world in future cycles of time	They may hope for the overcoming of the sickness of sin; for the continuance of man's being; and for the preservation of their life destined for eternity.
Amen	Yes, so it is

Steiner's reticence in explaining the Creed

In my view there is no doubt that Rudolf Steiner could have spoken for hours or even days about every single sentence of the Creed from the perspective of anthroposophic Christology. But he wanted to give the theologians the opportunity to make this text their own in thought and meditation, and later also in ritual enactment, and continually deepen their experience of it. Nor did he say anything relating either in principle or in detail to questions of translation other than what I quoted at the beginning. Only when reciting the first article concerning 'God' or the 'almighty divine being, spiritual-physical' did he allow himself a brief explanation:

> What we can say, drawing on spiritual science, is that the word 'God' points to something that expresses affinity, a relationship, and can be found in ordinary language in some dialects that contain the word 'God' ... and which we also find in the name Goethe whose original form was Goede. It signifies 'mentor' or 'godparent' – someone with whom we have a spiritual relationship.
>
> The word is intimately embedded in a monotheistic outlook, that of a great cosmic mentor whom we feel as a spiritual father by contrast to some arbitrary adviser or mentor. Thus the word grew out of primitive, monotheistic stages of religion, and in northern Asia was probably once called the *Ongod,* the one great godfather. This prefix *On*

certainly points to the monotheistic origin of ideas connected with the word God.

So you see, if you choose words with real inner conscientiousness, you cannot say them so easily and unthinkingly as people usually do today.

Continuing with his reading of the text section by section, Steiner then only sporadically referred to, and accentuated, the characteristics of his new version, such as the impossibility in relation to the Gospel of John of speaking of creation by the Father instead of by the Logos-Son ('I believe in the one God, the Almighty Father, maker of heaven and earth'). He also drew his listeners' attention to very precise use of the terms Christ, Jesus and Christ Jesus (instead of 'Jesus Christ') in the new text, but was otherwise very reticent in his comments.

Kurt von Wistinghausen reported that the theologians were by no means 'shocked' by Rudolf Steiner's new version of the Creed, but considered it 'very successful' or in fact far more than that: 'A decisive era had begun in a process of development lasting two millennia ... like a trumpet fanfare, [this text] initiates a whole new Christian era.' According to Adolf Müller, the youthful audience experienced in the new Creed the flaming up of 'a modern Whitsun spirit'. Just one year later, they came to Dornach again with only *one* question about the wording of the new Creed, asking Rudolf Steiner to explain whether, in article 4, the wording ought perhaps to be 'to heal spiritually the bodily nature of mankind from the sickness of sin'.* He answered:

---

* The North American translation of the Creed quoted here uses 'within the bodily nature'. The British translation uses 'of the bodily nature' which may not fully bring out the difference between these two versions. Steiner's version emphasises healing the sickness of sin that *inheres within* the human body, the question asked by the priests was healing the human body *from* the sickness of the sin. (Transl.)

What is meant is this: ... to heal spiritually the
sickness of sin that resides *in* the body. That is its
meaning. One might also say 'to spiritually heal the
bodily nature of mankind from the sickness of sin...'
But I would prefer to have 'in the bodily nature'.

On October 8, 1921, he had recited '[the sickness of
sin] *of* the bodily ...'; but henceforth *'in* the bodily' was
used in the Act of Consecration of Man in the original
German.

No doubt the theologians would have been glad to have
more explanations from Steiner. The transcript of the
meeting of September 17, 1922, has the comment 'More
information about the Creed is requested.' In his reply,
Rudolf Steiner responded to the written submission
to him about the formulation involving healing of the
'sickness of sin', but otherwise said this:

This Creed that I have given you has been drawn
from real spiritual perception. There is something
in the Creed that is different from the rituals. The
rituals are offered as something arising as the forms
of ceremony. In this Creed something is given that
embodies the confession of faith of a religious person
today. One can agree with it, or not agree with it ...
You may today be able to say that you have trust in
me having given you this Creed. You wish to declare
your agreement with this Creed today, and to regard
this agreement for the time being as consent to its
teachings. It is scarcely possible to raise any objection
to the Creed.

Shortly after this, he said, *'Otherwise I have nothing
further to say in relation to the Creed.'*

Actually Steiner could have said a very great deal in relation to the Creed; but he felt it necessary to allow what was 'spiritually inviolable' in it simply to stand there for the time being as it was, or to find resurgence in its new wording, thus enabling the priests to embark on their work. After ten years as a celebrant, Adolf Müller was to write in 1932:

> The other words of the Act of Consecration are apostrophic in character. Because all these prayerful sentences invoke the divine world, one can say that a personal relationship to the divine holds sway there. But in the Creed, the inner eye gazes up to luminous truths that embody the existence and action of the divine powers. Beyond the wrestling, yearning and encompassing of the divine that moves our souls in the entirety of the Act of Consecration, the revelation of the world of spirit shines out in the Creed. In its tranquil sublimity it resembles the heaven of fixed stars that arches over the ever-changing course of the planets.

Our responsibility today

Adolf Müller, who undertook such a profound study of these matters, said the Creed possessed *'the beauty and clarity of a crystalline configuration of Christian consciousness'*. He believed that with it, or with the healing and redeeming truths laid down in it, human dignity could be re-established anew in the twentieth century. According to Müller, the Creed makes a substantial contribution to the human incarnation and connection of Christ with human evolution and thus to what makes possible the 're-enlivening of dying earth existence'. The inner movement of the Creed requires heart forces, and indeed, *heart thinking* of a Michaelic nature. Adolf Müller experienced it as a 'foundation stone that must be implanted in the human heart'. He concluded his book with this phrase in 1932, a few months before the Nazi regime seized power and embarked on its rule of terror.

As we all know, survival of the 'intrinsically human' is today hugely endangered by manifest evil. The redeeming and healing power of Christ and the healing spirit are urgently needed today in all areas of culture and civilisation. The aim of 'wresting from the death of matter' people for whom this is possible 'through their bearing' is a very topical concern, but in the face of the global and excessively powerful sway of forces wedded to materialism, it seems scarcely achievable. It says in the Creed, in regard to Christ and the souls to be saved by him, 'those whom, through their bearing, he *can* wrest from the death of matter'. There is freedom here in that Christ's capacity to act is defined or limited by human 'bearing' or conduct. Everything depends on human beings themselves, but human beings are ringed about by powerful forces and powers of temptation, and live within their spell of enchantment. And yet Christ, the 'Lord of the heavenly forces upon earth', is very close to human beings in our era, which is also the era of the Archai Michael. With Michael's help, we can find the way from the kingdom of Ahriman (or even *through* the kingdom of Ahriman) to Christ.

In his essay on the Creed, Georg Dreissig pointed out that the return of Christ – in Greek, *parousia* – literally means 'existence' and 'presence'. Rudolf Steiner described the etheric return of Christ as 'the greatest secret of our age', and spoke of the raising of the human being into the realm of the etheric, which will enable Christ to become perceptible to us – specifically through the experience of misery and the abyss; of evil, in fact. But the Creed – as spiritual 'seal of the heart' (as St Ambrose called it) is of key importance for engaging with this whole process, which requires a great deal of courage and inner assurance. Georg Dreissig wrote:

> In the Creed we grow beyond our earthly humanity
> toward the Christ, indeed, we grow into him:
> our feeling insight and grasp of the secret of our
> humanity, which is rooted in God and his Creation,
> reveals itself ever more deeply, and at the same
> time becomes apparent in and through us. As we
> repeatedly look upon him and upon ourselves in the
> present era, we place ourselves into his presence.[13]

Christ entered the earthly world 'as human being',

as the Creed emphasises in its new version. 'Christ in the form of a servant' passed over the land, 'blessing it' during his incarnation, and is once again close to us, a brother to human beings, a counsellor and friend.

In this context, Andreas Laudert recalled Rudolf Steiner's unusual translation of the Caesarea Philippi scene, presented on March 7, 1911, in a lecture in Berlin on the Gospel of St Mark. Steiner said there that Christ did not (only) ask about himself but also about the human I and humanity altogether ('What do people say of the I?). And Peter replied:

> We understand the I in its essential spirituality to be you, the Christ![14]

'Communities whose members feel the Christ within themselves' in this sense form the I-community of the future, of the only possible future on earth, as we can say today after the devastating *and* renascent experiences of the twentieth century.

The Creed for the future

We need strong powers to develop these I-communities of the future: we need the powers of our own essential being and inner truth as expressed in Rudolf Steiner's Foundation Stone Meditation. The Creed cannot relieve us of the need to develop these powers, and it certainly does not have a magical effect, not even any more in its Latin form. But as a *'seal of the heart'* it also carries weight in the age of Michael. As Kurt von Wistinghausen said, it can become 'Christ's light in our daylight' and remind us of the foundations of our human existence and of our humanity. In its modern, anthroposophic form, it speaks of this existence, and not only of faith. 'An almighty divine being, spiritual-physical, *is* the ground of existence of the heavens and of the earth.' He truly is this, not only in my subjective religious conviction or faith. We can 'agree or not agree' with 'the confession of faith of a religious person today', as Rudolf Steiner said to the theologians, but we must respect it.

Georg Dreissig recalled that the Greek word for 'confession' – *homologeō* – literally signifies 'agree' or 'say the same'. The anthroposophic Creed is concerned with reality and not with belief – 'Yes, so it is'. It is entitled to be so because it describes the human being and the world 'as expressing themselves in and through us in a way that accords with the divine thought of creation,' as Dreissig put it. Against this background we can intimate why Rudolf Steiner said that the Creed was 'spiritually

63

inviolable' and, in September 1922, did not think there was a purpose in discussing it further. ('Otherwise I have nothing further to say in relation to the Creed.')

It would be interesting and enlightening to discuss Rudolf Steiner's version of the Creed in relation to Thomas Aquinas's exegesis of the thirteenth century, which was given fully in the spirit of the Gospels, the Epistles of Paul and patrology; or to contrast it with modern interpretations (such as those by Joseph Ratzinger or Hans Küng). All this however is beyond my remit here and would exceed the scope of this account. Instead I would like emphasise once again, at the end, that Rudolf Steiner regarded the Creed as an 'essence of cosmic wisdom, of all cosmic feeling and cosmic will,' and very consciously and specifically placed its new, spiritual version into the twentieth century, as something that was most urgently needed in this era of turbulence and upheaval.

I do not think that Rudolf Steiner initially saw the need for a renewal of the Christian rites, or even for a movement for religious renewal out of the spirit of anthroposophy. Many aspects of his work, by contrast, suggest that he regarded the era of churches and altars, acts of worship, of communion and of priests and ministrants, as having run its course. On October 9, 1918, he was still saying this: 'If the churches understand themselves rightly, they cannot have any other goal but to make themselves redundant on the physical plane by turning all of life into an expression of the supersensory or spiritual realm.'[15] There is a long list of similar comments. But then it became apparent to him that the world of spirit not only supported but *willed* a refounding of the rites of Christianity, and that people on earth did truly need this, as did other beings also. Rudolf Steiner's subsequent collaboration in the founding of

The Christian Community was active and committed, and without doubt he saw it as a contemporary need with high priority. His comment on May 17, 1923, applies by no means only to the movement for religious renewal but it does *also* apply to it:

> If you truly absorb the spirit of anthroposophy, you will find that it again opens human ears, human hearts and the whole human soul to the mystery of Christ.[16]

Participation in a renewed Christian cultus requires no prior conditions and can mark a new beginning. Likewise, no prior conditions whatsoever are necessary for understanding the new form of the Creed. We do not have to know the Roman Creed, the Apostles' Creed nor the Nicene Creed, let alone be familiar with centuries of theological and philosophical debate around the text in order to be moved and indeed profoundly stirred by this new Creed. As I said, Rudolf Steiner impressed upon the priests of The Christian Community the need for them to pursue studies of history and of the evolution of consciousness, but this by no means applied to all who can find a spiritual relation to the Creed. Steiner was in favour of the new wording being disseminated. As he said in his lecture in Basel on October 19, 1917, with which I began my commentary, 'The spirit of our age is moving toward openness, toward things being in the public domain, and anthroposophy, specifically, lives with and in this spirit.'[17]

Five years later, on September 20, 1922 – exactly nine years after laying the foundation stone of the First Goetheanum as a school of spiritual science in the era of evil – he emphasised likewise that 'The Creed must of course be made available to all congregation members.'

It is possible that in future the Creed will come to be of relevance not only for 'all congregation members' of The Christian Community but all human beings altogether who are deeply concerned with the 're-enlivening of dying earth existence', the 'preservation of their life destined for eternity' and indeed, with hope of a coming cosmic age. *'For the Son of Man came to seek and to save the lost'* (Lk 19:10). This 'healing power of the Christ' can also become available to those who have already died, and whose conditions during life meant that they could make only tentative first steps, or none at all as yet, to find their way out of Ahriman's spell and the 'death of matter'. They too 'may hope'.

The future of Christianity as the religion of humanity, but also the future of humanity altogether, is more uncertain than ever in our world today. But many people in many places, of different world views and religious faiths, see the importance of building spiritual community. 'That they may be one as we are one,' as Thomas Aquinas said in his commentary on the Creed, quoting the Gospel of John (17:22), and emphasising it with a quotation from Paul's Letter to the Ephesians (4:15f):

> Speaking the truth in love, we will grow to become in every respect the mature body of him who is the head, that is, Christ. From him the whole body, joined and held together by every supporting ligament, grows and builds itself up in love, as each part does its work.[18]

> *Communities whose members feel the Christ within themselves may feel united in a church to which all belong who are aware of the health-bringing power of the Christ.*

Notes

1 'Anthroposophie stört niemandes religiöses Bekenntnis' (lecture of Oct 19, 1917) in Steiner, *Freiheit, Unsterblichkeit, Soziales Leben*.
2 Steiner, *Building Stones for an Understanding of the Mystery of Golgotha*, pp. 39f
3 Steiner, *Approaches to Anthroposophy*, lecture of Oct 16, 1916, pp. 60f.
4 Steiner, *Vorträge und Kurse*, II, p. 444.
5 Wistinghausen, *Das Neue Bekenntnis*.
6 Unpublished transcripts from the Christian Community archives, Berlin.
7 Steiner, *Unifying Humanity Spiritually*, lecture of Jan 16, 1916, pp. 184, 186.
8 Gädeke, R. *Die Gründer der Christengemeinschaft*.
9 Frieling, Rudolf, 'Von den Ursprungskräften des Bekenntnisses', in Lindström, *Der erneuerte christliche Gottesdienst*, pp. 136–41.
10 Apuleius, 'The Ass is Transformed,' *The Golden Ass*, p. 241.
11 Müller and Suckau, *Werdestufen des Glaubensbekenntnisses*.
12 Fichte, *The Way Towards the Blessed Life*, lecture 1, p. 14, quoted by Johannes Lenz, 'Das Bekenntnis des Petrus', *Die Christengemeinschaft*, Jan 2010, pp. 20f.
13 Dreissig, Georg, 'Hinaufwachsen in das Offenbarungslicht Christi,' *Die Christengemeinschaft*, Jan 2010, pp. 6–10.
14 Steiner, *The Background to the Gospel of St Mark*, p. 138, quoted by Andreas Laudert, 'Sein Ich bekennen,' *Die Christengemeinschaft*, Jan 2010, pp. 17–19.
15 Steiner, *Death as Metamorphosis of Life*, p. 114.
16 Steiner, *Menschenwesen, Menschenschicksal und Welt-Entwickelung*, p. 134.
17 Steiner, *Freiheit, Unsterblichkeit, Soziales Leben*, lecture of Oct 19, 1917.
18 Thomas Aquinas, *The Apostle's Creed*, Article 9

Bibliography

Apuleius, *The Golden Ass* (tr. Robert Graves) Penguin Books 1950.

Fichte, Johann Gottlieb, *The Way Towards the Blessed Life* (tr William Smith) London 1849.

Gädeke, Rudolf, *Die Gründer der Christengemeinschaft. Ein Schicksalsnetz,* Dornach 1992.

Gädeke, Wolfgang, *Anthroposophie und die Fortbildung der Religionen,* Flensburg 1990.

Lindström, Sigrid (ed.), *Der erneuerte christliche Gottesdienst. Beiträge zu seinem Verständnis. Aufsätze 1929-1975,* Hannover 2002.

Müller, Adolf, *Werdestufen des Glaubensbekenntnisses: eine geistgeschichtliche Untersuchung,* Stuttgart 1932 (rev. ed. with Arnold Suckau, Stuttgart 1974).

Schroeder, Hans-Werner, *A Christian Creed: A Meditative Path,* Floris Books 1985.

Selg, Peter, *Christ and the Disciples, The Destiny of an Inner Community,* SteinerBooks, USA 2012.

—, *The Lord's Prayer and Rudolf Steiner: A study of his insights into the archetypal prayer of Christianity,* Floris Books 2014.

—, *Rudolf Steiner and The Christian Community,* Floris Books 2018.

—, *Rudolf Steiner and the Fifth Gospel: Insights into a New Understanding of the Christ Mystery,* SteinerBooks, USA 2010.

Steiner, Rudolf. Volume Nos refer to the Collected Works (CW), or to the German Gesamtausgabe (GA).

—, *Approaches to Anthroposophy,* Rudolf Steiner Press, UK 1992.

—, *The Background to the Gospel of St Mark* (CW 124), Rudolf Steiner Press, UK 1968.

—, *Building Stones for an Understanding of the Mystery of Golgotha* (CW 175), Rudolf Steiner Press, UK 2015.

—, Rudolf, *Christianity as Mystical Fact and the Mysteries of Antiquity* (CW 8), Rudolf Steiner Press 1972.

—, *Death as Metamorphosis of Life* (CW 182), SteinerBooks, USA 2008.

—, *The Fifth Gospel: From the Akashic Record* (CW 148), RSP 1985.

—, *Freiheit, Unsterblichkeit, Soziales Leben* (GA 72), Dornach 1990.

—, *Man's Being, his Destiny and World Evolution* (CW 226), Anthroposophic Press, USA 1984.

—, *Menschenwesen, Menschenschicksal und Welt-Entwickelung* (GA 226), Dornach 1988 (most of the lectures translated in *Man's Being, his Destiny and World Evolution*).

—, *Vorträge und Kurse über christlich-religiöses Wirken, II. Spirituelles Erkennen, Religiöses Empfinden, Kultisches Handeln* (GA 343), Dornach 1993.

—, *Unifying Humanity Spiritually through the Christ Impulse* (CW 165), Rudolf Steiner Press, UK 2014.

Thomas Aquinas, *The Apostles' Creed* (tr. J.B. Collins), New York 1939.

Wistinghausen, Kurt von, *Das Neue Bekenntnis. Wege zum Credo,* Stuttgart 1963.

Also by Peter Selg

Rudolf Steiner and The Christian Community

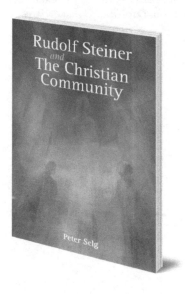

'The book is informative and enlightening on a subject
that, perhaps, is still not quite properly understood by those
within the anthroposophical movement, but ought to be.'
– *New View*

In this unique book, Peter Selg seeks to answer the often-asked
questions about the complex relationship between The Christian
Community and the Anthroposophical Society.

This long-overdue book is a significant exploration of Steiner's
legacy which should have far-reaching implications for mutual
understanding and cooperation between The Christian Community
and the wider anthroposophical world.

florisbooks.co.uk

The Lord's Prayer
and Rudolf Steiner

A study of his insights into
the archetypal prayer of Christianity

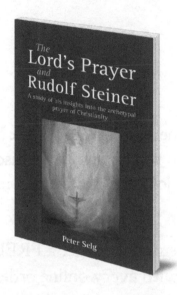

'This book, which is a gem, has the potential to become a companion for every human being, who is interested in the central prayer of Christianity and wants to open heart, spirit and mind for it.'
— *Perspectives*

Rudolf Steiner once called the Lord's Prayer the 'greatest initiation prayer', and he spoke about it many times, also referring to it as the central prayer of Christian experience.

This book is, however, the first time that all of Steiner's comments, accounts and perspectives have been brought together in one place, presenting the full scope and depth of his ideas. Along the way, Peter Selg reveals some surprising insights into the spiritual history and mission of Christianity.

florisbooks.co.uk

Floris
Books

For news on all our **latest books,**
and to receive **exclusive discounts,**
join our mailing list at:

florisbooks.co.uk

Plus subscribers get a FREE book
with every online order!